# My funny cat

## Bobbie Kalman

🌳 **Crabtree Publishing Company**

www.crabtreebooks.com

# Created by Bobbie Kalman

**Author and Editor-in-Chief**
Bobbie Kalman

**Reading consultant**
Elaine Hurst

**Editors**
Kathy Middleton
Crystal Sikkens
Joan King

**Special thanks to**
Jennifer King, Educational consultant

**Design**
Bobbie Kalman
Katherine Berti

**Production coordinator and Prepress technician**
Katherine Berti

**Photo research**
Bobbie Kalman

Photographs by Shutterstock

**Library and Archives Canada Cataloguing in Publication**

Kalman, Bobbie, 1947-
    My funny cat / Bobbie Kalman.

(My world)
ISBN 978-0-7787-9500-1 (bound).--ISBN 978-0-7787-9525-4 (pbk.)

    1. Cats--Juvenile literature. I. Title. II. Series: My world
(St. Catharines, Ont.)

SF445.7.K34 2011          j636.8          C2010-901969-5

**Library of Congress Cataloging-in-Publication Data**

Kalman, Bobbie.
    My funny cat  / Bobbie Kalman.
        p. cm. -- (My world)
    ISBN 978-0-7787-9525-4 (pbk. : alk. paper) -- ISBN 978-0-7787-9500-1
(reinforced library binding : alk. paper)
    1. Cats--Juvenile literature. I. Title. II. Series.

    SF445.7.K35 2011
    636.8--dc22

                                                                2010011295

## Crabtree Publishing Company

www.crabtreebooks.com          1-800-387-7650

Printed in China/072010/AP20100226

**Published in Canada**
**Crabtree Publishing**
616 Welland Ave.
St. Catharines, Ontario
L2M 5V6

**Published in the United States**
**Crabtree Publishing**
PMB 59051
350 Fifth Avenue, 59th Floor
New York, New York 10118

**Published in the United Kingdom**
**Crabtree Publishing**
Maritime House
Basin Road North, Hove
BN41 1WR

**Published in Australia**
**Crabtree Publishing**
386 Mt. Alexander Rd.
Ascot Vale (Melbourne)
VIC 3032

# Words to know

dance

have fun

laugh

play ball

read

sing (talk)

swing

wear flowers

3

I have a funny cat.

My funny cat likes to wear flowers.

My funny cat likes to talk.

My funny cat likes to have fun.

My funny cat likes to sing.

My funny cat likes to dance.

My funny cat likes to play ball.

My funny cat likes to read.

My funny cat likes to swing.

My funny cat likes
to laugh and laugh.

Do you have a funny cat?

What does your funny cat like to do?

# Notes for adults

### Objectives
- to allow children to share their fun experiences with pet cats
- to learn about cat behavior and interacting with pet cats
- to teach children the infinitives of verbs

### Before reading the book
Write these words on the board:
my, funny, cat, likes, to
Ask these questions: "Do you have a cat?"
"What are some things that all cats do?" (walk, run, sit, talk, purr, meow)
"Does your cat like to play with you, or does it prefer to be alone?"

### Questions after reading the book
"Why do you think this book is called *My funny cat?*"
"What are some of the things the cats in the book like to do? Do you think these things are funny?" (wear flowers, talk, have fun, sing, dance, play ball, read, swing, laugh, hide, ride a bike, kiss a frog)
"Which of these things do cats really do? Which things do cats not do?"
"What things do cats do that dogs do not do?" (climb trees, use a litter box, meow, pounce, stalk)

### Activity: Learn about wild cats
Read the book *Baby Cats* to the children.
Ask the children these questions:
"What other kind of cats are there?"
"What are wild cats?"
"Who looks after wild cats? Who looks after pet cats?"
"How are wild cats different from pet cats?"
"What do they eat?"
"Which wild cat has stripes?" (tiger)
"Which wild cat has spots?" (leopard)
"What sound do big cats make?" (roar)
"Name a big cat that roars loudly." (lion)
"What sound do little cats make?" (meow)

### Extension
Read the sentences from *My funny cat.* The words "like" and "likes" are followed by the word "to." Bring the attention of the children to the infinitive of verbs and ask how else they could say the same sentence. i.e. "likes dancing, likes singing," etc. Ask them to say each sentence in this different way.

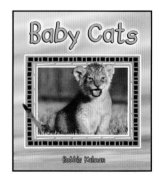

This book is part of the ***It's fun to learn about baby animals*** series.
***Guided Reading: J***

*For teacher's guide, go to www.crabtreebooks.com/teachersguides*